John Kirk

Britain's Drawbacks

Second Edition

John Kirk

Britain's Drawbacks
Second Edition

ISBN/EAN: 9783744690140

Printed in Europe, USA, Canada, Australia, Japan

Cover: Foto ©ninafisch / pixelio.de

More available books at **www.hansebooks.com**

BRITAIN'S DRAWBACKS:

BEING

A BRIEF REVIEW

OF

THE CHIEF OF THOSE NATIONAL ERRORS WHICH
RETARD THE PROSPERITY OF OUR COUNTRY.

BY

REV. PROFESSOR KIRK,
EDINBURGH.

SECOND EDITION.

GLASGOW:
CHRISTIAN NEWS OFFICE, 142 TRONGATE.
EDINBURGH: A. MUIR, COCKBURN STREET.
MANCHESTER: UNITED KINGDOM ALLIANCE OFFICES,
41 JOHN DALTON STREET.
1868.

NOTE.

The following pages are published at the request of some able and influential public men, and will, it is hoped, lead to sound thoughts on some momentous subjects.

GLASGOW: PRINTED BY H. NISBET, TRONGATE.

BRITAIN'S DRAWBACKS.

It cannot fail to be both interesting and profitable for a people to consider those matters that retard, or that render all but null and void, their efforts to reach lasting prosperity. By doing so they may hope, not merely to regret, but to remove the evils which so seriously affect their progress.

We propose in this Paper to look somewhat carefully at *five* different aspects of that incubus of error by which British enterprise is affected. Our country *seems* to go backward; if it does not really do so, it sadly fails to go forward; and it appears to us that there are five great lines of popular belief, along which we are declining as a people.

The first of these aspects of mistaken faith—which at least hold us in check—presents itself in the *position of labour*, as at present represented by the great organisations of working men. Every one knows that, naturally, the end of labour is *production* —that is, the great natural aim of all labour, strictly so-called, is to produce that which is necessary to the sustenance and comfort of mankind. It can scarcely escape notice by the most unobservant that the produce of labour is exclusively the substance of material wealth. Man has nothing earthly worth having which is not the result of labour. Capital, which may or may not be represented by money, is only a name for the gathered produce of toil.

For illustration, let us imagine an island having, say, sixty inhabitants—men, women, and children. Only a very limited number of these can be productive *labourers*, in the proper sense of the word. Thirty at least will be children, or old persons equally with the children incapable of such labour. Ten more ought to be wives and mothers, totally occupied with the care of the young, and old or sickly among such a people. We may lay out at least five more as among the idle or disabled in one way or another. It will be a favourable state of things if, in such a community, we have *fifteen* really producing labourers, whose toil will feed, clothe, and shelter themselves and all the rest in the island.

It must be seen at a glance that the more these fifteen produce, consumption being the same, the richer will that people be; and that the less these produce the poorer they must be. Nothing can be more clear than that, if we regard nature as seeking the greatest good of all, the natural aim of these labourers is to produce as much as they possibly can, consistently with their continued efficiency as labourers. Nor is it less clear that, if they aim at the greatest wellbeing of themselves and their fellow-islanders, they will draw every hand they can rightly enlist into productive labour. The greatest possible wealth of the people, as a whole, is just the greatest possible accumulation of produce; and, seeking that wealth, these men will do their best every way to increase production.

It will be well to observe that *money* may not be required so far as such a community is concerned. There must be labour on the one hand, and produce on the other: nothing more need be considered in connection with the common wealth of the islanders. We select such a case for illustration, because it simplifies our point of view, and sets the one subject of productive labour clearly before us.

Let us then suppose that these fifteen men take it into their heads that the less they produce the better! They shorten their hours of toil, and refuse to allow more than a very limited number of young lads to learn to labour! Their grand aim becomes, not to increase as far as possible, but to diminish as far as possible, the food, clothing, and shelter provided yearly for the community ! They somehow imagine that in this way they will benefit themselves, their wives, and families ! The less ground tilled, the less sown, the less reaped, the fewer fish caught, the less cloth woven, or flax or wool grown, the less stone quarried, and the fewer houses built in a season, so much the better ! What would be the issue ?

But suppose that they not only think the less produced the better, but also the more destroyed the better too ! They invent, we shall say, some means by which a very large proportion of all the grain they raise shall be effectually put out of reach as food, and so that the store for common use shall be thus far reduced. In view of this large deduction from their actual wealth, they flatter themselves that somehow their riches are increased ! What must the issue be at length with the community, should such delusion hold its ground ? *Famine* will be the inevitable result.

Suppose still further that this destruction of grain is for the sake of a drug which induces laziness and recklessness in those labouring men who use it. It makes them every way less fit for productive toil, and far more wasteful of produce. Will not *famine* come speedily? This famine will show itself first in the case of the weaker and less cunning of the people. Certain strong and clever individuals will be able for a time to secure a far more than equal share of what is actually produced and spared from destruction in the aggregate of all that is provided for the mass. But certain others will have by that much less than their share. And as the whole produce will be below the mark, even if each had his full share, the poor will be poor indeed.

Now there will be poverty-stricken children, old persons, sick and otherwise disabled persons, and very soon their state will become so serious as to *force itself* on the attention of their more fortunate brethren. There will be such suffering that the comfort of the more fortunate will be destroyed by the terrible condition of those below them. Men will be compelled to say to one another that "*Something must be done.*" This is the birth of that terrible scourge of a deluded people, which we style "*pauperism*"—not the poverty of the naturally poor, but the pauperism *necessarily following* the restriction of productive labour, and the destruction of produce.

But these wise labourers may still think it best to restrict production, and to destroy, or allow to be destroyed, an increasing amount of produce ! They now agree that help for the poor shall be levied from the islanders at large. As matter of fact, however, this help can come from those only who are in a position to furnish it—that is, from the ten or twelve most able producers, who are really all in the community who can have anything to give. With this poor rate the beggared class must be fed and otherwise provided for ! A very powerful and increasing means of limiting production and also of consuming produce is now supplied by this pauperism. This, no doubt, compels all classes to admit the importance of the productive labourer. The "*bread-winner*" is an object of no mean regard to a starving family. But no amount of such regard will add a loaf to the store. The industrious and frugal in such a case must support the profligate till they are helpless to do so. The truth is, that society in such pauperism has begun to eat itself up, not like the serpent, by the head swallowing the tail, but by the tail eating towards the head !

But this is only a faint picture of our own land as the anomalous position of labour presents it to view. No secret is made of the fact that the great Trades Unions aim at restricting production as far as it is possible to do so. This is the result of a state of mind brought about by such a combination of errors as must ever issue in a similar popular mistake. In that state of mind the abstraction called "*labour*" has taken the place of the concrete reality, which exists only as the *produce of labour*. The vast working class now speak, not of produce, but of labour as merchandise. The "labour market" is the accepted phrase with them—not the produce market. They sell *labour*—not produce. It is their interest, situated as they are, to sell their labour at as high a price as they can have for it; and in order that they may do so, they must restrict as far as possible the supply of labour in the country. The number of hours for labour must be shortened; apprentices must be made as few as possible, that there may be a small supply of labour, and hence as urgent a demand for it as may be! Like any other merchant weighing out his goods for a certain price, the workman must carefully weigh out his toil, and give as little as possible for the money. That means that there shall be as little production in the country as it is possible for the producing classes to secure by means of indefinite restriction. It surely cannot require much skill in thinking for any one to see that this must make the community poor as a whole, and that just the further it is carried out every one in that community must ultimately be the poorer.

There is, as might be expected, some important utterances on this subject in Mr Gladstone's remarks on Trades Unions, lately addressed to the deputation that waited on him. He says (we think strangely)—" With regard to the principle of associations among working men, with a view to the diminution of the amount of labour, and getting the best price for it that it will bring in the market, I can take no exception to that principle." From this sentence, it looks as if Mr Gladstone were quite pleased that working men should combine to *diminish labour*—that is, to restrict production! But he says again—" I own it appears to me as a general rule that regulations in restraint of labour go to diminish the aggregate amount of the fund which constitutes the whole wages of the country." Would he then, *in the interest of working men and their families*, take no exception to *a principle of association which goes thus to impoverish the commonwealth?* Is it right for any body of men to combine (even for the purpose of enriching themselves) so as to impoverish the whole community? May they do this forcibly and at the cost of their weaker brethren? We shall suppose a trade into which a certain limited number of apprentices only are admitted, and a considerable number excluded. Have the members of that trade a right to make their own wages unnaturally high, by keeping others from adding to the general store of good, and also from getting any wages at all ?   Or have they a right to limit production in this way and impoverish the community, merely that they may have a larger share of the limited produce than naturally falls to their lot ?

But it is not necessary to dwell on the *right* of the case.   Is it *possible* thus to raise wages *permanently?*   All wages, like wealth of every possible material kind, depend upon the amount of production among a people.   It is gross absurdity to imagine that true wages depend upon *money*.   Apart from produce money is worthless.   Place a man on a desert island, and give him a million sovereigns in gold, and how long will it keep him alive ?   Place him where it will require a quarter of a million to buy food for a week, and he will live just four weeks and die the fifth.   Make produce *scarce* and you raise prices ; that is, you make money, whether in the poor man's hand or in that of the rich man, worth so much less.   Diminish labour and you diminish production ; thus you make prices rise—that is, you lower the value of money.   You may use that money as the price of produce, or you may use it as the wages of labour—it must really be used as both ;—but when its value is lowered, it is just as truly lowered in the one case as in the other.   When you thus succeed in lowering its value, no doubt you make the rich *less wealthy*, but you *make the poor still more poor*.   The rich have generally real property, such as houses and lands, to fall back upon.   They may reserve their money for a time, but the poor are compelled to buy for life.   The rich are affected, but the poor are beggared when the value of money is seriously lowered.   Does Mr Gladstone take no exception to combinations of men for this express purpose ?   May men raise their own wages by thus forcibly restricting the general good ?   Will they do this and escape impoverishment themselves ?   They will just as really leap into the fire and not be burned !

For the sake of a very clear illustration of this, we may look to the case of cotton manufacturing machinery in Lancashire at present, as compared with that of Belgium.   In England machinery is scarce, and its price high ; elsewhere it is plentiful, and its price low. Let us say that a manufacturer has £10,000 to lay out in this way. That money is equal to £11,725 if spent in Belgium, though the goods bought have to be transferred to this country. By sending money there for his machinery, the manufacturer makes himself £1725 richer than if he spent it in Lancashire. Englishmen, by restricting labour, and specially by waste of produce, have brought about this anomaly. There is a better way. The landlord of a large temperance hotel told us lately that he had sought in vain for sober waiters till he sent to Germany for them, and now he had a full set perfectly free from the liquor vice. It would not be difficult for British workmen to compete with those of any country if our producers were thus free.

It is utterly vain to think that we can confine the area of productive labour to our own island by any combination that can possibly be formed, even if the British Government itself should be foolish enough to join in the union. There was a time when owners of land thought to limit the area from which food might be grown for British subjects to these narrow lands, and they succeeded for a season in inflicting untold misery; but an irresistible force of national growth and necessity broke through the barriers, and stretched the area over the world. What the owners of land could and could not do, is just the same as that which owners of labour can and cannot do by restriction. They can inflict untold misery by a temporary diminution of the country's wealth, but they cannot long confine their fellowmen within bounds beyond which God has determined they shall go. A workman said to us, lately, that, by combination in his trade, they had forced up their wages farthing by farthing in the hour, and he was evidently greatly satisfied with the result. But he forgot that, as they had been so forcing up their wages in Britain, money had been here falling, in its relative power to buy, far faster than their wages had been increasing; and hence that his class, instead of rising in the social scale higher than their fathers, had been coming down. Could the working men be got to unite to save the vast amount of produce now worse than wasted, and to increase the available wealth of the country as far as possible, so that the wages which they should then receive would purchase double the amount which they purchase now, there would be cause for congratulation. Could things be got to that pass, that £100 would purchase as good a house as £200 will do now, even if wages were lowered fifty per cent, the man who needs such a house would be the gainer.

It is vain to storm at a man who buys in the cheapest market, or at one who sells in the dearest, whether the money he seeks is in the way of wages or of profit. But it is of very great moment indeed that all should keep the real character of the money question in view. It should never be forgotten that it is the relative and not the nominal value of wages which enriches the workman. Their relative value depends upon the amount of produce in the market of the world. If that amount is *low*, the relative value of money is also low; if that amount is *high*, so is the relative value of money. If one shilling will buy as much as a man can consume in a day at one time, and it requires two shillings at another time, money is only half the value at the latter time that it was at the former. A man with one shilling a day is as well off at the one time as he is with two at the other. So if at another time he pays four shillings for that which could be bought formerly for one, he is not a farthing better with four shillings for a wage than he was with one. Now, in so far as men lessen production and diminish the value of money, they raise the nominal but lower the relative value of wages. Is it wise then to combine for this very purpose? If a bricklayer may do so wisely, no doubt a farm-labourer may do so likewise. But is it wise in either? It is neither right nor wise. It is a contest with the very nature of things, and men may just as well associate to compel *yes* to be *no*, as they may associate to raise actual wages by the restriction of productive toil. They may please themselves, and others may please them by asserting that they are poor because there is too much produce in the country, and that they will be far better off if they can make it less; but such absurdity has to be paid for in hunger and nakedness in the long-run.

It must ever be kept in mind in connection with the limitation of productive labour, that a very serious deduction is made from the amount of it in the country by the vast number of men whose employments are utterly unproductive. The whole army—the navy—the police—the revenue officers—with the vast multitude engaged in manufacture and trade of such a nature as adds nothing to the sum of available subsistence—these must be added to the great numbers who live to consume only. All these are necessarily subtracted from the productive classes, and yet consume more produce in proportion to their numbers than the producers themselves. Taxes and expenditure on what are called "luxuries" and "amusements" represent a large portion of actual produce which is thus consumed. The nation is poorer by all this consumption, having no compensating production, but could easily bear the loss were not that loss aggravated, as it is by our present system of liquor licence. We might almost dispense with prisons and police were it not for this, and with a vast proportion of other labour of an unproductive character.

It should be kept in mind, especially by the working man, that the great mass of unproductive humanity must be fed, clothed, lodged, educated, and made comfortable, if he and his should starve! It must be attended to, come what will to the productive labourer. This is the fault of no man—it is a law of society that no human power can reverse. The labourer does not know as he sits by his fireless hearth in hard times that he and his family are without bread entirely because the non-productive mass is so unnaturally increased. He is unaware even that those who make no additions to the general store are fully supplied, while he has nothing. Ought he not to look into the cause of this anomaly, so as to consider that, were the great drink system put down, the non-producing class would be reduced by nine-tenths?

But the labourer is fool enough even to *dread this!* He actually thinks it is better that he should work to feed other men, than that they should work for themselves!! He imagines that if our vast prison and police force were to find their occupation gone, there would be such competition in the "labour market" that wages must fall!! So he prefers to work for the police and all others rather than let them compete with him for toil!! Surely it does not take a great amount of *brain* to enable one to see through such folly. Half a head might be able to see that, if one man works to feed himself and his own family, with the addition of another man and his family, his position in the nature of things must be worse than if he laboured to sustain himself and his own family only. But no,—men do not see it! They will have it that they are better to have a large non-producing class and a small producing one!! " *Wages*" are their snare. They cannot, or will not, see beyond the mere money! The less work others do the more is left for them!! They forget that *all must eat*, even if only very few labour, and that the labouring few *must* (in spite of all theories) *feed the whole.* This is worthy of the most earnest consideration of the rich, as it is of that of the labouring classes. As non-productive millions increase in number, property of every kind in the land *must fall in value.* These millions consume it, as we have said, in defiance of all law made by man. We can just as easily shake ourselves clear of our own being as we can shake ourselves clear of them.

A great effort is now being made to diminish non-productive labour by cutting off a proportion of the trading class. Co-opera-tion means nothing more than this as an economical principle. Men resolve to employ their own servants in trade instead of allowing other men to do this for them. So far as they can successfully do this, they shut out the men who have hitherto employed trading hands. In so far as trading talent is called into play among co-operators they will succeed in their enterprise, and this real addition to trading power will be a gain to the general community. In this way they may compel a portion of the trading class to become labourers in this or in other lands, and so they will achieve a limited gain to the general good. They will probably compel a portion of the smallest traders to go on the poor roll, and this will be a deduction from the good. But all the gain thus secured will not sensibly affect the great growing stream of pauperism which is so fast doubling its proportions in society. The profits of co-operation will prove a mere *mite* in comparison with the gigantic expenditure of the great drink system. If all trade were made co-operative to-morrow the gain would not touch, far less compress, the vast maw of beggary that is devouring us.

Before we go further, it may be well to introduce another aspect of error in our country's condition—that which is seen in *trade*. It is not the natural aim of the trader, strictly so-called, to *produce ;*—it is his to *distribute* that which has been produced by labour. And here it is well to remember that it is the produce of labour and not labour itself which is the natural merchandise of the trader. Labour, apart from that which it actually produces, is worth nothing. If, for example, a labourer cuts a drain in a field, it is the drain alone which is worth anything to any one. It matters not whether this drain is cut in a day, or in a week, or in a month of toil—it is the drain that alone is of any value. It is the drain which this labourer actually sells for so much, and which the man who employs him buys at that price. It is not the labour. But the drain is produce, and not merchandise. The payment for it is wages, not profit. The two things are distinct in nature, and should not be confounded in thought. The workman is paid for what he produces, and for that alone—the trader is paid for the transfer of that which he brings within reach, though it has been produced by another.

To illustrate this, we shall say that two of the labourers on our imaginary island are enterprising men, and they build a good vessel, such as may carry them and a cargo safely to another island at some distance from their own. Their own island has excellent timber, admirably fitted for building purposes ; that other island has none, but a great abundance of coal, which is far better fuel than the timber, but is useless for rafters. These men take away a cargo of good trees, and bring back one of good coal. If they produced all the timber, and maintained themselves and families at the same time, then the coal is all their own ; yet the island is wealthier for this transaction. The coal will soon find its way among the people, in exchange for other produce, and increased comfort will be the result. Such is the natural aim of sound trade. These men produced, it may be, neither the wood from the forest, nor the coal from the mine; but if they only brought these products of labour to the several places where they were required, they increased the available general wealth. That increase of wealth gives them a claim on their fellows, and their reward is represented by their profit on the exchange.

It will be at once seen that it is only in so far as there is enriching produce to exchange that there is scope for true trading. If production is restricted and produce destroyed, so must trading, strictly so-called, be restricted. In the same proportion as these islanders curtail produce, in that same proportion will they limit the cargoes, to and fro, of their little ship, and so keep down the wealth of the community. A "strike" of miners, or of iron workers, in this country necessitates the lying idle in port of many noble vessels, and as certainly curtails the national resources. This is lost sight of when labour instead of produce is considered capital; but the nature of things does not bend to human forgetfulness. Restricted labour, which means restricted production, not only restricts trade, but also the wealth which traders bring.

And yet there is one way in which restricted labour fosters trade, and in which trade takes the proper place of labour. Traders at present sailing between England and Belgium, go, it may be, with ballast only, and bring back machinery. A small cargo, worth, say, £10,000, gives, as we have seen, a fair profit of something like £1725. In this way the trader supplies the deficiency caused in Lancashire by the restriction of produce; he, in fact, takes the place of the labourer, who should have produced abundance of machinery on the spot. So far the trader saves the commonwealth from the ruinous efforts of the restrictionist. This is natural trade, but unnaturally called for! It is in favour of prosperity and not against it, so far as it is considered in itself, but the opening for it arises out of a ruinous state of things.

Now, we must consider the effect of unnatural trade. We have not in this country to contend with the restriction of productive labour only. An almost inconceivable amount of produce is given in exchange for that which is in itself a curse instead of a benefit. Let us suppose that our islanders give their traders a large cargo of substantial food, and get back a cargo of intoxicating liquor. Here is a double evil. The wealth of the island is lessened by the amount of produce sent away; but it will also be lessened by the amount of hindrance to labour which the liquor will occasion. They have restricted production—they now encourage trading which robs them of a large portion of the limited produce, and brings a certain large increase to their pauper class! And they regard this as a most satisfactory mode of life! Such procedure will bring great suffering first in the weaker portion of the population; but then, as we have seen, these soon turn upon the stronger, and the community, as a whole, begins to decline. As we have said before, the tail eats back towards the head, till the guilty race disappear from God's earth, which their presence dishonours.

The extent to which productive labour is diminished by the influence of the drink system is incredible. We received a statement from a foreman as to the effect on the wages of working men under him. He took a case from the wages book as a fair average specimen, and gave it as follows:—During eight weeks before taking a pledge of abstinence, the man's average weekly earnings were £1 6s 9½d; during eight weeks when keeping the pledge, £1 14s 4d; during eight weeks after breaking the pledge, £1 6s 10½d. Here is a loss of wages equal to 7s 6d per week; as near as may be, £20 a year on one man! If we consider the comparative inefficiency of the man, the loss to society is far greater; and if we add the sum spent by such a man on the liquor itself, it is not difficult to see how pauperism must soon overtake both him and his. A master, who at the time employed 6000 hands, told us that the lessened amount of labour caused by drinking, was so enormous that he really did not know what could be done with the hands if the license system were put down! He half thought with Trades Unionists that it would be calamitous if men and women should set their hearts on doing as much good to the world as they easily might accomplish! But when the vast mass now involved in our liquor system proceed on the principle of loss and waste, so rapidly increasing, there are issues coming on society as a whole which will cure such absurdity.

We may give a vivid illustration of this principle at work. There are about 200,000 inhabitants in Edinburgh, including Leith. It would be a high estimate to say that there are 25,000 working men among these. There is one distillery in the city, causing an outlay of above £50,000 a-week. If the weekly produce of the 25,000 men were worth £2 each man, here is an expenditure that swallows up the whole, giving in return only liquor, infinitely worse than worthless! Give 25,000 men £2 a-week each to go about horn idle, and the wealth of the community would be vastly less reduced than it is by this expense! Such is one great element of trade in relation to labour in this country,—and the relation of labour to that trade we have seen. But what is the inevitable issue? *Pauperism.* The weaker portion of the community must give way before the pressure of inevitable want, and as our civilisation insists that they shall die only gradually and decently, we are compelled to pass sweeping poor laws, to build gigantic workhouses, and so to find that poor-rates and misery are increasing in an alarming degree.

A great effort is now put forth to equalise the burdens of local taxation. This is nothing more than the uneasy burden-bearer shifting his load from one shoulder to another. It eases for a time; but, as the burden is increasing now, the relief cannot be for long.

But here, perhaps, it is well to consider that aspect of our national error which takes the form of *government.* As the natural aim of labour is to produce—and the natural aim of trade to distribute production—so the natural aim of Government in this relation is to encourage all that tends to the wealth of the nation, and to discourage all that tends to its poverty. We use the words "wealth" and "poverty" in their widest sense, yet as looking chiefly to material riches and their absence.

The ruling class in a nation which seeks its own enrichment, at the expense of the nation's impoverishment, has ceased to be, properly speaking a Government, and has become a trafficking, if not a swindling, concern. If, for example, in our supposed island, one man should be chosen to rule the rest, and he should consider chiefly how he might secure the largest share of produce to himself and his family alone, he would fail to merit the name of ruler, and deserve that of oppressor instead. If a very large share of the gain made by the trader, when bringing liquor instead of good produce to the people, were handed over to the so-called ruler in the name of "revenue" and he were so enriched in proportion as his people were being ruined, he would merit not their reverence, but their curses. If he appeared zealously to punish all that liquor occasioned on the part of the people, yet made his chief wealth out of its sale to them, he would stand convicted before God and man as a hypocrite and a knave.

It is probably saying that which is only too dreadful to be credited when we direct attention to the position of our rulers in relation to our country's greatest drawback. Of the £50,000 a-week laid out on drink in connection with the magnificent distillery already mentioned, not far from £25,000 go to the British Government! Liquor that can be produced so low in value as to sell at one shilling and threepence a gallon, is charged ten shillings a gallon of Government duty!! This is levied on the "proof" gallon, which goes out to be watered and "doctored," so as to bring the liquor trader something like twenty shillings at last!! Instead of discouraging the vast outlay, which is more than the entire wages of all the working people in the city, our rulers take about a half of the money! They compel the erection of workhouses, with the support of a rapidly degenerating and increasing pauper class. They do not lay out one penny of revenue in supporting the pauperism caused by liquor, nor do they give a farthing of it to make good the losses occasioned by the same. They only enrich themselves to the extent of some £12,000,000 a-year through the money which is caught from this very class as they are launched into ruin!

Some say that in speaking of the vast average sum of £25,000 a-week, we forget the drawback on exported liquor; but they, too, forget the vastly increased duty paid on that liquor when it is again brought back as bad brandy or rum to this country! We are not exaggerating the robbery, but putting it in the mildest form at all compatible with truth.

It is remarkable how easily society as a whole are deceived as to the progress of things in this respect. We constantly hear good easy souls, who are too easy to take the trouble of thinking whether a statement is true or false, saying that matters are greatly improved of late years. In 1856 the police took 2,768 persons off the streets of Edinburgh in a state of intoxication. In 1866 matters had improved so much that these officers had to remove 4,123 in the same condition! Is not this improvement with a vengeance? What must be the blindness which allows men to talk about improvement in such a state of things? The police touch no man, however drunk, if he is either able to keep his own feet, or can be dragged along by his more capable companions. The cases mounting from 2,768 to 4,123 in ten years, are those of persons utterly incapable of managing themselves. These are but a small portion of the class whose ruin enriches our governing classes.

But mark how the matter turns upon them. The successful traders, and especially the successful traders in the robbery of the vast labouring class, hold as their property that which is the produce of the labour of the masses. These masses feel that the produce of their toil cannot now be theirs. It is seen, as if inevitably, to pass into other hands. For example, the houses built by our artizans are not their own—the vast produce of their industry has passed from them—they get barely food and drink, with scanty clothing and shelter. They are left with nothing to sell but what they call their "labour." If they produce much, they are not the richer—if they produce little, they imagine they can be no worse, but may get more money, and be perhaps better. But do as they will, the liquor shop and enhanced rates of all sorts swallow all up, and leave them with nothing but this labour to take to market. Their position is a false one. It causes that they have no interest in property, strictly so-called. They are interested in "labour" only. The property, which is the product of labour, passes out of their reach while they are in the act of producing it. It passes, too, without bringing anything that can become property in return.

We had occasion lately to glance into a matter which illustrates this point. We were commissioned to look out for a villa in the suburbs of Edinburgh suitable for the residence of some friends from a distance. Going among the numerous dwellings erected for such residents, we were not a little interested to find the very large proportion of them that belonged to spirit dealers, and the still larger proportion in which they had been erected from the profits of the liquor business. Property worth many many thousands, now rushing up all round the city, can be traced directly to the till of the low liquor vault, at the door of which, if you observe for a few minutes, you see the producing classes going in and out by the dozen. The poor deluded men are going out toil-worn to the suburban districts from their crowded dens in the city, and building palaces for other men, taking the wages they receive back to those very men at their counters; so that literally they have nothing for their labour in the end but liquor! The men who successfully play on their gullability have the palaces—they have still only their dens! They are the victims of a system of *licence* that would be a disgrace to the government of Theodore the grim himself!

It is vain to speak of "improvidence" in this labouring class, when licence is given to do the worst that can be done to induce them to be thus improvident. It is known perfectly that if you open a public house in any community whatever, the result will be the "improvidence" of a certain portion of the population. If you open two such places, the "improvidence" will be increased. Our rulers suppress gambling; and, so far as this is concerned, they "force men to be good." But they licence liquor dealing in return for £12,000,000 a-year, taken from those whose improvidence is the direct result of that licence! What must be the issue with the labouring classes?

If their wages are high, the liquor vender is profited, but not the
labourers. If a time of stagnation comes in trade they are helpless. Their "labour" is then worth nothing, and all it has produced is the property of others. Is it any wonder if they combine
in defence of the rights (as they call them) of "labour"? Their
position entails upon them a continually increasing distress. A
war expenditure, such as gives them great prosperity, is necessarily followed by the collapse which war must ever bring. The
restrictions of productive labour by "strike" and kindred means
inevitably bring poverty to the classes who possess property, and
so make "labour" less in demand. "Hard times" come like death
itself to those who have nothing in the world but labour to eat,
when labour will not sell. Is it wonderful that the combinations
of men so placed become formidable even to the Government
itself? Is it not certain that, with a state of things like the
present going on increasing, such combinations will, by-and-bye,
prove a source of peril such as will make the stoutest hearted
quail?

When speaking of government, it is well to remember that the
vast and increasing criminal class are a fearful burden on the
shoulders of productive labour. The enormous share of national
wealth which goes to uphold our judicial and prison system,
together with our police and military so far as required by crime,
added to the support of the criminals themselves, is all a deduction
from that which is produced by the skill and labour of the fruitful
classes. In proportion as this vast drain increases, the power of
our labouring men to compete with other nations inevitably
declines. Government repression, coupled with Government
licence in this matter, is rapidly hastening on national ruin.
Results will show this soon, as words cannot.

In the case of Edinburgh, in regard to which we have infor-
mation of a reliable character most readily at hand, there are
some striking facts which illustrate how repression, such as it is,
grows into a huge burden on the community. In 1851, the yearly
salary of a superior officer of police was £93 9s—it is now £139
6s; that of a sergeant was (weekly) 17s—it is now 25s 6d; that

of a constable was (weekly) 12s 8d—it is now 20s 6d. From 1861, the fines taken in the police court have risen from the yearly average of £2254 to that of £4944. The police cases have *risen* 120 per cent., and the fines are *rising* at the rate of £1106 a year! The draft upon the resources of society threatens to swallow up everything. But this is not the worst feature of the case. The repression itself is as near as possible a delusion. A vast proportion of the police force, it is beyond doubt to those who know the real state of the case, are the servants of the liquor sellers rather than of the authorities. They must all be this, so far as the removal of incapable persons are concerned; but they are this in the way of allowing the law to be systematically set at defiance. No man need have any difficulty as to the proof of this if he has eyes to see anything, and goes from eleven o'clock at night till two or three in the morning within sight of the places where roaring drunkenness is going on, under the very guardianship of the officers of police. The fines imposed, large as they are, can be perfectly easily afforded as the share of profit handed to the police for allowing the illicit traffic to go on! The profits of a few nights, in some cases of one night, will defray the fine and costs, so that, perhaps, two or three months of sale may proceed unmolested. The vast profits of this traffic are corrupting our "repressors" from the crown of the head to the soles of the feet, just as ignorance and folly are devouring the toiling millions.

It is humiliating to see how the great bulk of those who are most deeply interested refuse even to look at the greatest of all causes operating against national prosperity. Speaking lately to an intelligent working man of the overwhelming waste of wealth in the liquor business, he jauntily replied, *"Oh, the money never goes out of the country."* The liquor trader has this consolation, with a very considerable addition. To him the money not only does not go out of the country, but it goes, in the first instance, into his pocket! The ruling class may also say that the money does not go out of the country, but into pockets from which they know how to extract it! The farmer and landlord, whose grain is destroyed, console themselves that the money does not go out of the country, but that a considerable share of it becomes theirs! But are not all classes deceived when they reason in this way? Do they not forget that money, as we have already shown, is worthless, except in so far as produce exists, for which it may be exchanged? Is not the working man specially deceived? We shall say that the money does not go out of the country (though this is very far from true when that country is becoming actually poorer in produce). We shall only hold that production is restricted, and a vast amount of produce destroyed. Everything becomes high in price—that is, money is lowered in value. It soon takes twice as much money to buy food for a family as it took before. The half of the money available has not gone out of the country; but it has virtually disappeared from existence. A loaf that was a penny is twopence, so twopence is worth just what a penny was worth formerly. Unless the rich man now consents to expend his wealth twice as fast as he did before, the poor man must inevitably find that labour is less in demand, and that, too, by the very fact that wages have risen. The money has not gone out of the country, but it has fallen in value from a cause that makes it inevitably evident that the change would have been a far less calamity if the money had gone abroad. That which money brings has become *scarce,* and no power of man can prevent that the pinchings of want shall be felt somewhere. They must be felt where money is not, and where *produce* has been consumed as it came to hand; but they will sooner or later be felt where wealth is greatest. It requires only a sufficient number of hungry stomachs in a country to make even its princes at last suffer want.

Now it may be well to glance at that aspect of error which is shown in the *philanthropic* efforts of the nation. It is not possible that so much indescribable misery should abound among any people as abounds among us and no efforts be put forth to mitigate it. So we have an incredible amount of such effort. Perhaps in no part of the wide field are our drawbacks more visible than they are here. If we look to the case of the city of Edinburgh, of the state of whose poor or "*lapsed classes*" a most able report is on the eve of publication while we write, we

find the number of these set down at the terrible figure of
45,030 ! This is only an approximate estimate. From the
report it would appear that the number is at least 66,000. As
Leith is not taken into the account, and 170,444 is the whole
population of Edinburgh, there are above a third of the entire
inhabitants of the city that are sunk into something like abject
misery!' In 1530 single-room houses, there are from six to
fifteen persons living in a single apartment! This population,
too, is increasing at an astounding rate, in defiance of all
efforts to mitigate the state of things. Is it any wonder that
men are becoming alarmed ? Is it not time that they learned
the truth—that is, that we are no longer concerned with this
matter as one of pity for others, but as one of self-preservation ?
From the last report of the Board of Supervision, we learn that
the amount required for the pauperism of the country was
£807,631 5s 6½d, or a rate per cent. on real property of
£8 13s 3½d. In 1847 the rate was only £4 13s. Let us observe
what this means. A farm, we shall say, lets at a rent of £1500
a-year. The pauperism of the country reduces that rent by £130
8s 4½d ! If this reduction is allowed to go on at its present
increasing ratio, it will swallow up the whole wealth of the nation
in a comparatively few years. Men may well be alarmed. Since
1816 the rate per head of the population has risen from fourpence
three farthings to its present rate, which is *five shillings per head!*
In Edinburgh as much as *thirteen shillings a-head* is raised for the
poor ! In this boasted city every tenth person is a pauper !
Instead of mitigation in the state of the poor from this amazing
rise, there is a vastly increased misery. The great thing now
with men of property seems to be the desperate effort to saddle
as much as possible of this terrible burden on each other. The
landlords in the country have pulled down every possible house
in which a pauper could lodge, that they might drive the helpless to the towns. Now the great men of the towns are agitating
for a law to equalise the rates and make all pay alike ! Mean-
time the vast monster grows apace !

Our philanthropic agencies and organisations are on a
scale truly vast. "City Missions" are to a great extent not so

much religious as simply benevolent in their character. They labour to clothe the naked and to feed the hungry, to cure the sick and to employ those out of work, even to find houses for the houseless. Our ragged schools are not so much for education as for the maintenance of poor children. Our sanitary movements, now engaging the energies of our most powerful men, are all of a benevolent character. Our temperance societies are innumerable, and all benevolent. There are multitudes of the indications of an earnest struggle against the misery that so terribly abounds. Yet the most resistless evidence crowds upon us, and demonstrates that all is nearly in vain. Police and prison expenditure increases; the poor rate increases. The demand for "refuges," "asylums," and "institutions" in which to accommodate the disabled masses, is constantly increasing. The amount of public beggary seems appallingly to increase. It cannot be otherwise. The devouring monster of our liquor trade swallows up far more than all that charity can provide to meet the constantly increasing want. That which charity provides in the shape of clothing goes almost directly into hands for which it is not intended. It goes at first to the poor wretches that seem so terribly in need, but they carry it to the pawnbroker, and it is sold by him to another class who have money, though not much of it, to buy. A large portion of it is sent to Ireland, where, though the people generally are poor, they are not pauperised as we are. There is one pauper only in 120 in Ireland, but more than one in 10 in Edinburgh. That money which is advanced on the pawned goods goes at once to the liquor seller. It only increases the amount of liquor consumed by the destitute.

All our plans of benevolence have this sad defect—they deal with far off symptoms, while they leave powerful causes of misery untouched. As a consequence, *they fail to prevent the increase* of misery. We are deeply concerned to see the way in which the report already mentioned deals with the great liquor curse. It says—"All available and judicious means should be employed to protect the poor from temptations to form habits of drunkenness." Again—"Our whole licensing system requires reconsideration, and some principles laid down to guide those with whom the responsibility of granting licences lies." It is nearly incredible that men with the very slightest notion of the real state of things, should imagine the slightest possibility of improvement in our lapsed masses with a licensed liquor trade kept on among them! Above 60,000 men, women, and children, mulcted of the last possible penny that pawns and drink can take from them, are to have the liquor sold to them still; but nevertheless "all available and judicious means" shall be employed to protect them from temptation! How men will make fools of themselves!

A temperance society reclaims perhaps a dozen in a year, say, of intemperate persons, while a single spirit dealer out of thirty in the same district teaches a score to drink and to become rapidly intemperate. The remaining twenty-nine liquor dealers do their full share in providing superabundance of work for the temperance men. When will such benevolence stem the tide of misery? A Dorcas society clothes, say, fifty poor people; but a single pawnbroker will gather to his shelves in the same time as much as strips two hundred! And there are, at least, half-a-dozen pawnshops for every such society! When will this process banish the rags and nakedness of the poor? A reformatory gathers up say a hundred young rascals that are caught one way or other in petty thefts; but one-tenth of the liquor dealers in the field from which the reformatory has its inmates will make more than as many into criminals in the time the reformatory cures half its hundred! When will this overtake our growing crime?

There is an incredible loss which arises out of drunken pauperism of which few comparatively are aware. Certain medical men, and no doubt certain men who have liquor to dispose of, think it necessary to supply our sick poor with enormous quantities of liquor. In two workhouses in Edinburgh as much as £353 12s 5½d was spent in the space of one year in liquor supplied for the paupers! In the same year, £77 15s were laid out on tobacco and snuff for the inmates of those houses!! In all, £431 7s 5½d in two out of the three Edinburgh workhouses!! In one month (ending February 14th, 1867,) 96 bottles of whisky were supplied to 88 persons and 36 bottles of wine to 41 persons in the City workhouse! *Twenty* of the patients so treated died within the month! In one workhouse clothes were disposed of by the inmates to the amount of £358 in the space of fourteen months. Inmates were clothed in new suits—scaled the walls—went "on the spree"—came back naked —were clothed again to go again on the same errand—were clothed a third time to do the same. After all, they were *forced* back on the workhouse by Sheriff's order, or by that of the Board of Supervision! When these model men had done service to the utmost in this way, they were sent to jail, still to be well fed and clothed at the productive man's expense! Should not productive labour and wealth know that all this has to be paid for, either out of current production or out of the hoarded store? Every one suffers for this but the successful liquor vendor and a few non-producers. They have the robber's share. Ought men to allow themselves to be hoodwinked to all this by the silly prejudice against "extreme temperance views"?

There is an almost incredible amount of philanthropic effort expended on classes on whom the great liquor curse has got no hold. Beginning with "*Savings Banks*" and going on with a vast number of other similar remedies, certain benevolent persons imagine that they are reforming the poor. We wonder how many of the 60,000 persons in Edinburgh, who live in one room in sixes and even in fifteens, have money in the Savings Bank? How many of them will ever have a penny in even a "Penny Bank" if the liquor system holds on among them? We are exhorted to go among these masses to reclaim them, because the frightful increase of assessment for the poor without any mitigation of the evils of poverty, is alarming thoughtful men; but we are to go on the understanding that the grand, lucrative, respectable traffic in pawns and liquor is to keep its ground! Can philanthropy be more terribly caricatured?

We may look now to that aspect of our country's error which shows itself in matters of *religion*. The grand element of true piety is supreme love to God, and love to our neighbour equal with that which we bear to ourselves. The grand motive to this love is the self sacrifice of God in Christ for the guilt of mankind. In view of this religion, nothing can live which conflicts with the interests of any human being. It goes to the very root of all social wrong.

But how stands the religion, actually professed in this country, in relation to that country's worst and most ruinous wrongs? It is wedded in the closest of unions with the greatest of all our curses. The most universally acknowledged of our Christian men—noblemen, gentlemen, and ministers of the gospel—are enriching their families by the liquor traffic. They do so openly, and it does not in the least degree tarnish their Christian fame. It is no disqualification for the highest and holiest offices of religion to owe one's wealth and position in society to successful brewing, distillation, or liquor-selling! That which is making paupers by the thousand, and eating the heart out of the nation's prosperity, is thus nursed in the warmest part of the bosom of the Church! How then can religion help us out of our sad situation?

If we look at these drawbacks on our country's prosperity in the aggregate, we cease to wonder that men of thought are becoming puzzled and alarmed at the progress of things. Labour irresistibly combining to keep production low—trade labouring to destroy produce and still more reduce production, so as to make prices high—Government enriching the ruling classes on the profits of the most ruinous of all traffics—benevolence itself playing into the coffers of the pawn-shop and tavern—religion, above all, rearing her temples and paying her ministers from the wages of iniquity! Is it astonishing that men who love country and kindred are brought to their wits' end?

Where is the remedy for all this? We reply that no remedy is possible which does not imply that men shall learn to love their neighbours as they love themselves. Every shred of that system—*principle, if you will*—which implies that you shall have more if your neighbour should have less, must be torn off and thrown to the winds, or the people may make up their minds for an earthly perdition. All classes must combine for the benefit of all, or God shall as soon cease to be God as he will either give or allow our deliverance. The ruling power in the nation, whatever that may prove to be, must take hold of the destructive selfishness now in action, and strangle it. St George must slay the dragon again, or the dragon will devour the nation. There must be courage enough found to tell those men—who think they have not only a right to be idle themselves, but to order others to be idle also, and who claim to diminish production in order that wages may rise—that the right they claim is that of robbery, and must be dealt with as such. There must be pith enough in the moral force of the nation to put the foot of suppression on traffic which is fitted only to degrade and ruin the people; and pith enough, too, to show the formal Government of the day that it must repress instead of fostering the great source of our social misery and degradation. Philanthropy must adopt common-sense and banish sentimentalism. It is infinitely absurd to do as has not unfrequently been done when the collector of a temperance society calls upon the liquor seller for a subscription! Above all, religion must learn to shake herself clear of her union with human wrong. A great change is before us, and now close at hand, when the legislative and ruling power is to pass into more numerous hands. We must wait to see the result; but if we are not merely to get deeper into the mire, all classes that have their heads above water must unite to put down the great source of the present state of things, and to build up that barrier of social wealth to which every true son of his country is proud to contribute.

APPENDIX.

The following summary of an admirable lecture, by Councillor David Lewis, of Edinburgh, may form an appropriate addition to the foregoing pages :—

(From the Edinburgh Daily Review.)

COUNCILLOR D. LEWIS ON THE SOCIAL CONDITION OF THE COUNTRY.— Last night, Councillor David Lewis delivered a lecture to a crowded audience in Brighton Street Chapel, on "The Social Condition of our Country a Source of National Peril." Mr Lewis devoted special attention to the ravages produced by intemperance and the drink system. Taking our own city, for instance, it was a startling fact that 45,000, or one-fourth of the population of Edinburgh, belonged to the lapsed masses, including the criminal, the abandoned, and the poverty-stricken. With regard to the first of these classes, out of 9345 persons who passed through the hands of the police during last year, 4123 were under the influence of intemperance; and in the first month of the present year, 450, out of 650 who passed through the police cells, were taken from the streets in a state of intoxication. Then it was reckoned that there were 1500 unfortunate females in the city. Within the last 22 years the pauperism of Edinburgh had increased from 6387, or one in every twenty-one, to 20,607, or one in every ten; and it could be clearly demonstrated that nine-tenths of the pauperism was directly or indirectly associated with drink. Twenty-two years ago the entire expenditure for the maintenance of the paupers in this city was £21,172, last year it was £53,561, and evidence went to prove that not only had the people been pauperised by the drink system, but the money given them for maintenance was again expended in liquor, and went directly into the pocket of the liquor vendor. He had been told on the highest authority that the money might as well be transferred in one cheque to the publican, so directly did it go to him; indeed, the police knew the pay days of the Parochial Boards by the number of paupers in a state of intoxication. Such was the condition of Edinburgh, and it was only a type of the rest of the large cities in the empire. Thirty years ago there were 79,429 paupers in Scotland—now there were 255,580; and the consequent expenditure had increased from £155,000 to £807,000. Yet we talked of our country being a model of patriotism and philanthropy, while we were spending nearly a million of money annually in the support of pauperism, nine-tenths of which was really and truly preventible. Mr Lewis proceeded to consider who are the parties responsible for this state of matters. He accused the Government of violating one of the fundamental principles of the Constitution, as laid down by Blackstone, in permitting and licensing a calling which was adverse to the interests of the commonwealth; and he charged the Church with culpable neglect of its duty in being to a great extent silent on this important subject. With things in their present condition, we were as a nation drifting backwards, and our position was one of imminent and terrible peril. The sin of our country in relation to this matter would inevitably be visited with heavy national punishment. The drink traffic, legalised by Government and upheld by the Church, stood in the way of every social, moral, and sanitary reform; and he counselled, as the only true remedy, that all who had their country's welfare at heart should unite in order to sweep the system, in every branch and department of it, from the land.

We may add to the above an abridged report of a speech by Mr Lewis in the Council, on the 10th of March of this year. He says—
"Reference had been made to the shebeens, and he would tell the Council that the state of the city in this respect was most appalling and discreditable to us as a civilised and Christian people. The

poor people came to him in dozens, complaining and asking if the Council could do nothing to put down these shebeens. The other day a woman came to him and told him that her husband, who makes 28s or 30s a week, was in the habit of coming home at three o'clock on Sunday morning, and gave her 12s or 14s. Sometimes he went out again, and returned home half-stupified with drink, demanding 5s more ; and last week he had told her that he would have her heart's blood if she did not give him her last farthing. Another case was that of a man making 25s a-week, who came home at five o'clock on a Sunday morning with 2s 3d in his pocket. The Forbes Mackenzie Act had been grossly misrepresented in Edinburgh. He found that Mr Linton would not endeavour to get a conviction, unless he could prove an act of sale. This was not right. The Act showed plainly that if they could find drink in one of these shebeens, and if they could find individuals drunk or drinking, they were entitled to seize not only the drink and the occupants, but also the frequenters of the house. This was not done in Edinburgh, though it was done in Glasgow. Captain Smart, of the Glasgow police, says—'The magistrate does not require proof of sale of spirits on Sunday. Two things are necessary to insure conviction—first, that the house is known to be a shebeen ; and, secondly, that persons other than inmates are found there drunk or drinking.' Why not so in Edinburgh ? At the present time the enforcement of the law in Edinburgh was a perfect mockery. There were dozens, he might almost say scores, of public-houses open till twelve o'clock, and some were carrying on a roaring trade at that hour. Why was this ? If there was efficiency in the police staff, why should this go on ? Would any one who saw people reeling out of the public-houses at eleven or half-past eleven o'clock, in a state of gross inebriety, say this was a right thing ? The Council ought to confine this evil within the smallest possible limits, and not allow it to set the law at defiance. What we really wanted was a body of men to supplement the police, to go down into these jungles of sin and immorality—the shebeens—and to enforce the law ; not men to walk about the streets in a semi-military style, but to give effect to the law, and prevent crime from being developed to such an enormous extent. (Applause.) He thought that the operation of the law in Edinburgh was too much of a repressive and too little of a preventive nature. On Sabbath the 16th of last month, between the hours of one and four o'clock in the morning, no fewer than 45 persons were taken out of four of these shebeens, and carried to the police office. He asked the Council to think of the enormous amount of labour entailed by this means on the police, who had to spend hours in taking these 45 individuals into custody, while the public property they should have been watching was left comparatively defenceless. He had, along with the detectives, visited shebeens, and he found in some instances that not only were the doors secured by chains and locks, but they were covered with solid iron plates outside and inside, and bound with iron bars, and guarded in such a way that it would almost require artillery to carry the place. Were the Council, he asked, to sit still and take no action in the matter? It was poor economy to talk of the few thousand pounds of fines obtained out of those dens of wretchedness and degradation. When they considered the 4100 people taken from the gutters and put into the cells in a state of drunkenness, in the course of a year, could they fathom the terrible amount of suffering and degradation which this represented?"

Some most important statements by Thomas Knox, Esq., one of her Majesty's Justices of the Peace, merit much earnest attention, though published some years ago. We abridge a few of his telling remarks from a lecture of his, delivered on the 29th of April, 1865. Mr Knox says that—

"The first pawnshop known in Scotland was started in Glasgow in 1806, and proved a dead failure. The sign of the first three balls was as unwelcome to the then careful, forethoughted, and independent Scottish people as would any day be the sight of three devils. Another adventurous one, however, tried the experiment and succeeded, about the same period, and that one has literally become a thousand; for it is computed that of big pawn and wee pawn establishments, more than a thousand flourish in Scotland, working social and moral havoc unspeakable. It surely is, then, a very ominous fact indeed, that from none or one in 1806, we have reached a thousand in 1865! It is still more ominous, when placed alongside of another fact, that the poor-rates of Scotland, from being infinitesimally small in 1806, are now close on a million pounds sterling in 1865. Such facts are trumpet-tongued; and I say solemnly and earnestly, he that hath ears to hear let him hear what such facts proclaim of reproof and warning alike to Church and State—to Christians and politicians. In Edinburgh we have 33 licensed pawnshops, and 219 wee pawns or brokers—252 in all, gnawing into the very vitals of civilization, virtue, and religion. In the 33 licensed pawnshops alone—for only with them do I purpose dealing to-night—there are effected annually, and admitted by pawnbrokers in the columns of the *Mercury*, 1,881,200 pledges, high and low. High pledges and low pledges are a statutory definition of amounts pledged—all below 10s being a low, all above 10s a high pledge. The business done monthly in Edinburgh in low pledges, under 10s, is 110,000; high pledges, under £10, 5,000; and deposits above £10, 100. The nature of the pledging is seen by a peep into the interior of an every-day establishment. The list embraces the following articles:—Body clothing—men's coats, 539; vests, 355; pairs of trousers, 288; hats, 60—total, 1,242. Women's gowns, 1,980; petticoats, 540; wrappers, 132; duffles, 123; pelisses, 90—total, 2,865. Pairs of stockings, 84; silk handkerchiefs, 240; shirts and shifts, 294—total, 618. Bed clothes—bed ticks, 84; pillows, 108; pairs of blankets, 262; pairs of sheets, 800; bed covers, 162—

total, 916. Miscellaneous—table cloths, 86; umbrellas, 48; bibles, 102; watches, 204; rings, 216; Waterloo medals, 48—total, 654:—sum total, 6,195. If we divide the 1,381,200 of such pledges in Edinburgh, we will find that each place effects as near as possible 41,000 annually, or 8,500 monthly. But some of these establishments transact an almost incredible amount of business. I have it on the best authority that one office in a poor district, betwixt the Castle and Holyrood, effected in one month 11,000 pledges! All the 11,000 were low pledges, sums below 10s, with the exception of 30, which were high pledges, above 10s. This surely reveals a social condition among the poor of Edinburgh that needs very special attention and treatment. I have had the most harrowing interviews with working men, almost driven to despair and madness about their families, in consequence of wives pawning, with ruinous facility, everything during their absence at work. One man told me that his house was stripped of everything, his daughters were unable to cross the door—their mother having stolen and pledged their things while they slept, and that unredeemed pledges were lying in the house in 'goupons!' I have seen strong men literally broken down with grief and starvation, large wages being consumed by pawnbrokers and publicans. Allow me, also, to give you a brief narrative of other authentic cases—a mere sample of hundreds more—from the private diary of a gentleman whose extensive intercourse with the poor gives weight to his words. A working man, earning all the year round 18s per week, has a wife and children. His wife is given to intemperance, and takes fearful rounds of drinking. He does everything in his power to keep her from getting drink—keeps the money and means out of her way—pays all the accounts himself, and does everything he can to prevent her drinking; but all utterly fails on account of the facility given to such characters by the pawnshops. I have known her three or four times strip the children and herself of clothes, leaving just rags enough to cover them, and empty the house of everything she could carry away—the bed clothes, the clock, and pictures from the wall—the very pots and pans; and when all such things are gone, in desperation she breaks open every lock in the house, and leaves nothing. I have known her poor husband, week after week, have to take the shirt from his back, wash and dry it on Sabbath, that he might have it clean to go to his work on Monday. When all in the house is gone, then she goes to the clubman, gets £1 or £2 worth of cloth in her husband's name, with the promise to pay it at so much a week. Of course her husband never sees it, it goes straight to the pawnshop; and the first notice that he gets of it is months after, when his wages are arrested for the payment of it. The husband is kept from church, the children are kept from school —they have to sleep without bed-clothes, and live almost without body-clothes; and for all this the pawnshop is much to blame."

All this is going on with aggravations to the present hour.

www.ingramcontent.com/pod-product-compliance
Lightning Source LLC
Chambersburg PA
CBHW021453090426
42739CB00009B/1740